YOU CAN DRAW
ZOO ANIMALS

by Jannie Ho

PICTURE WINDOW BOOKS
a capstone imprint

MATERIALS

Before you start your amazing drawings, there are a few things you'll need.

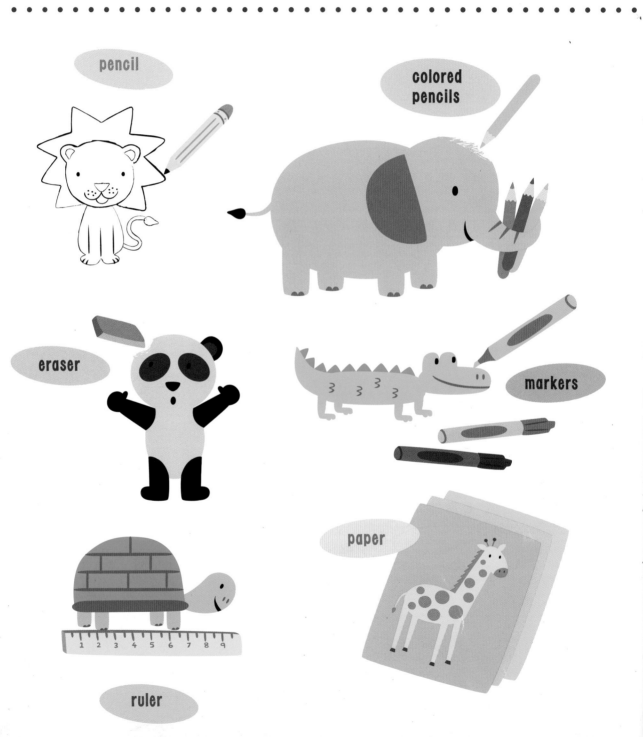

pencil

colored pencils

eraser

markers

paper

ruler

SHAPES

Drawing can be easy! If you can draw these simple letters, numbers, shapes, and lines, YOU CAN DRAW anything in this book.

letters

A B C D
T U W

numbers

1 2 3

shapes

lines

Polar Bear

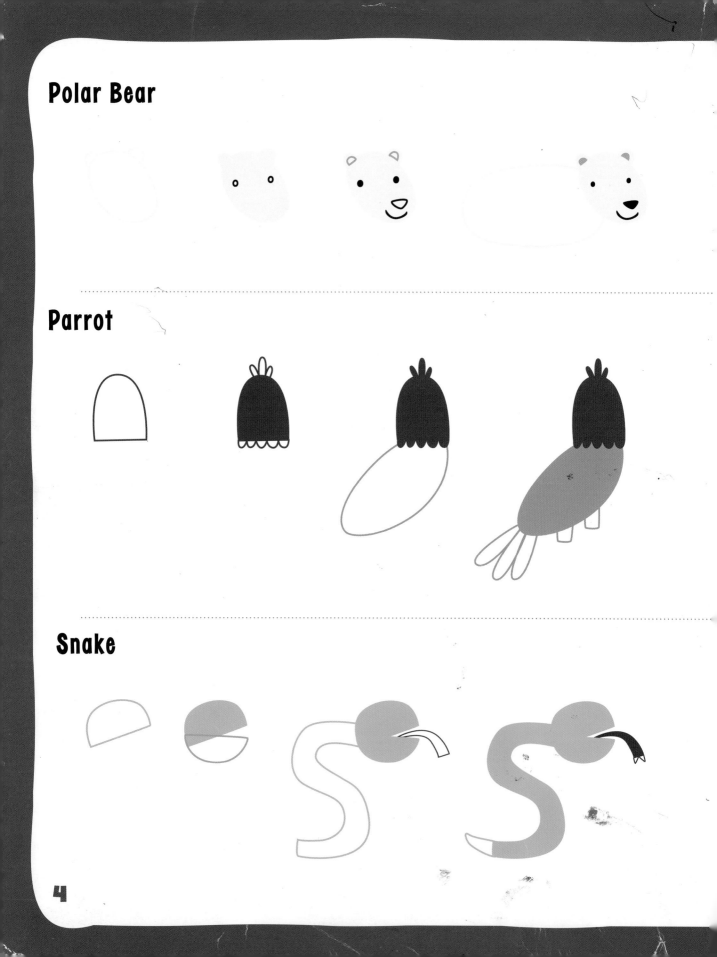

Parrot

Snake

4

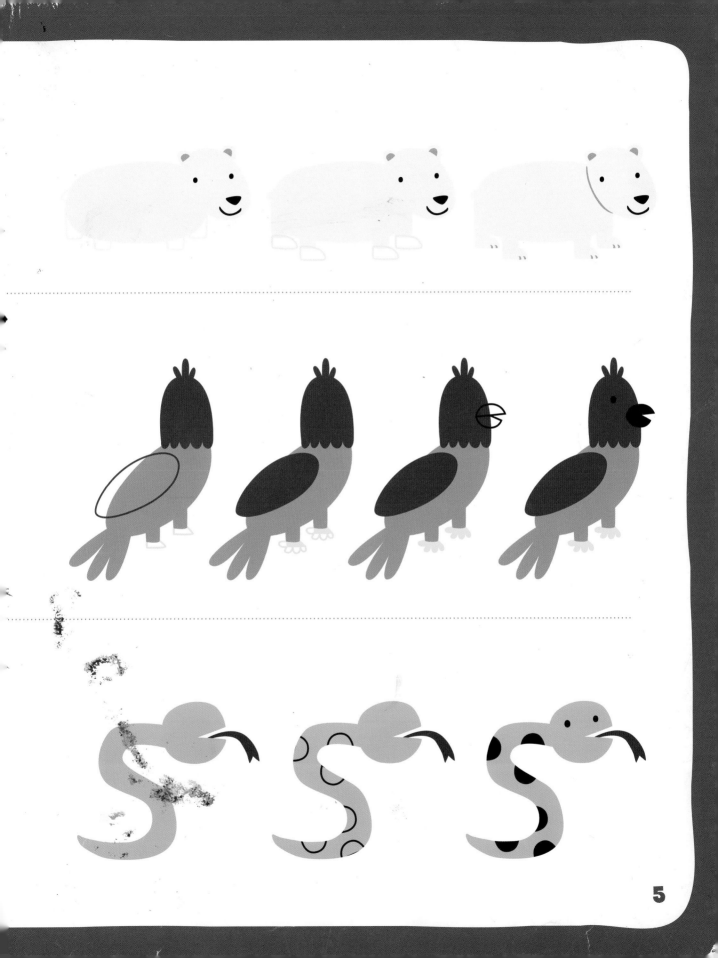

5

Zebra

Elephant

Ostrich

7

Penguin

Crocodile

Kangaroo

Tortoise

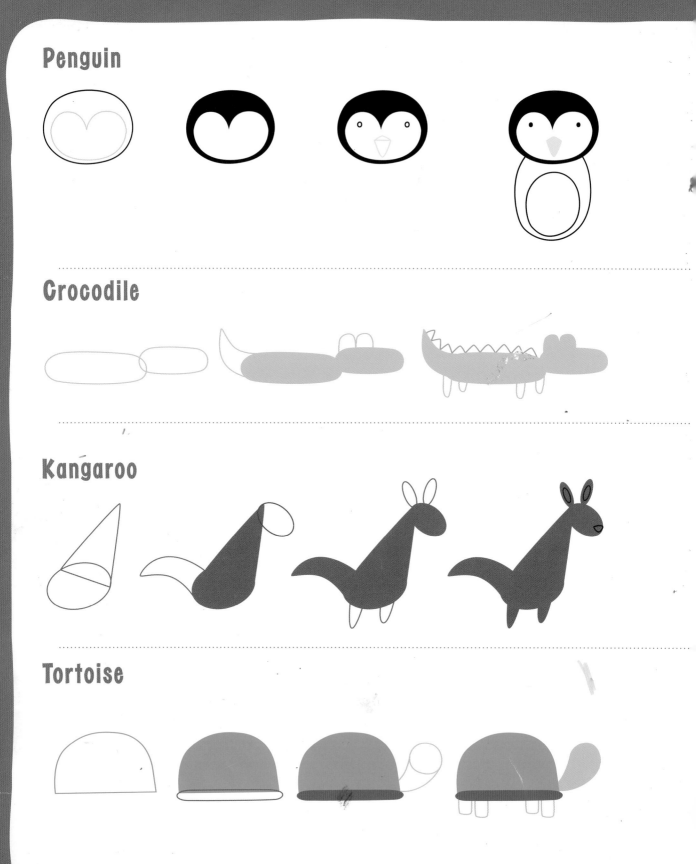

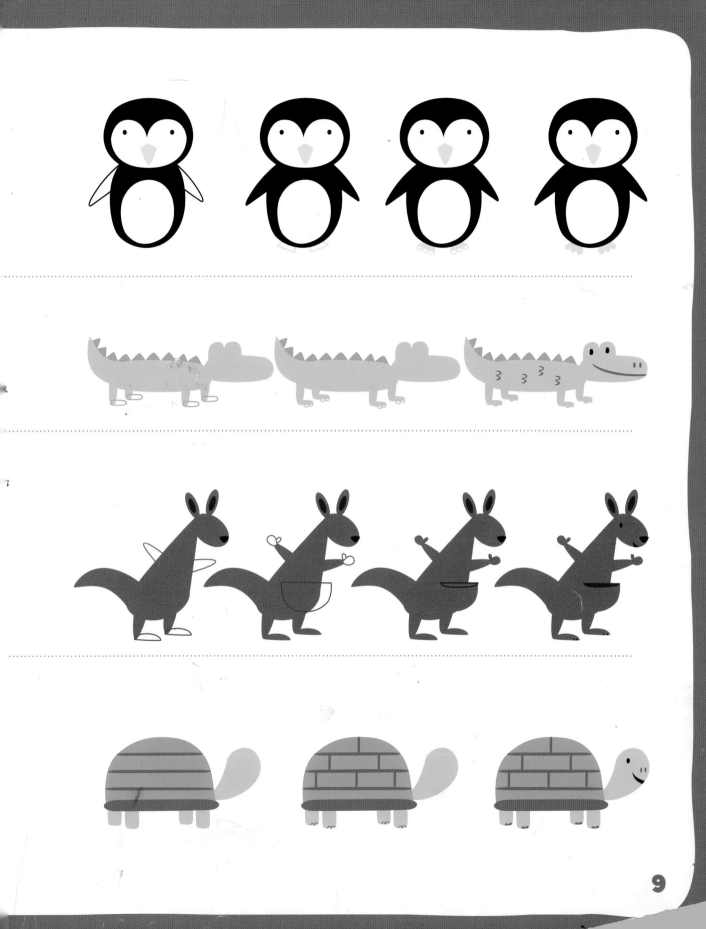

9

Lion

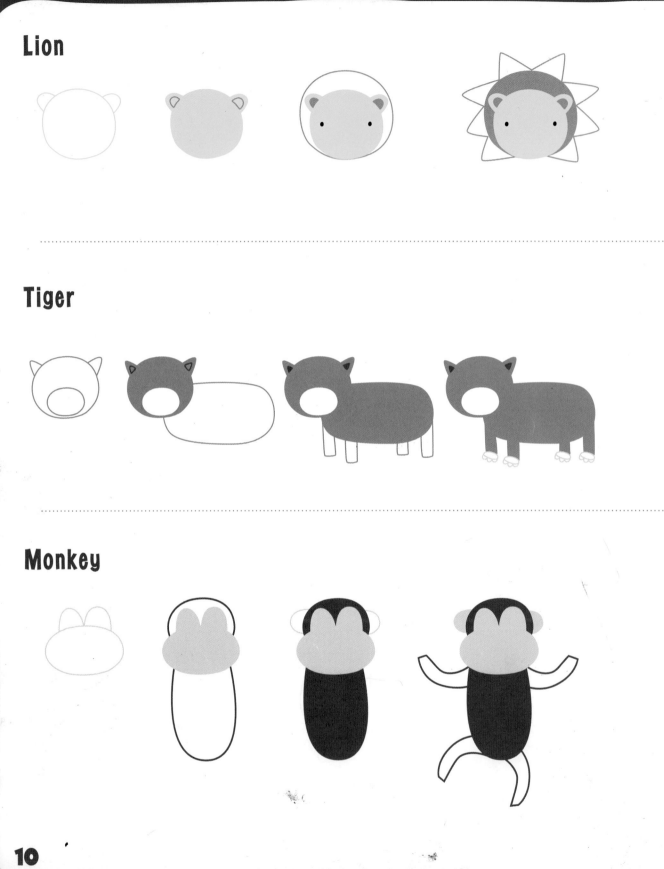

Tiger

Monkey

11

Whale

Hippo

Shark

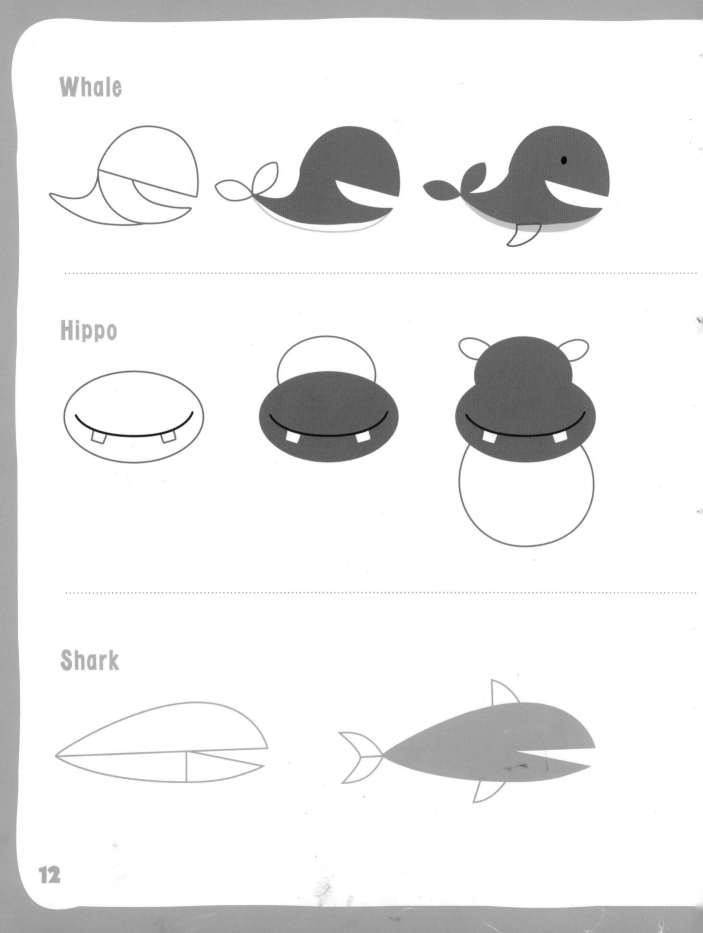

Giraffe

Anteater

Seal

15

Llama

Panda

Prairie Dog

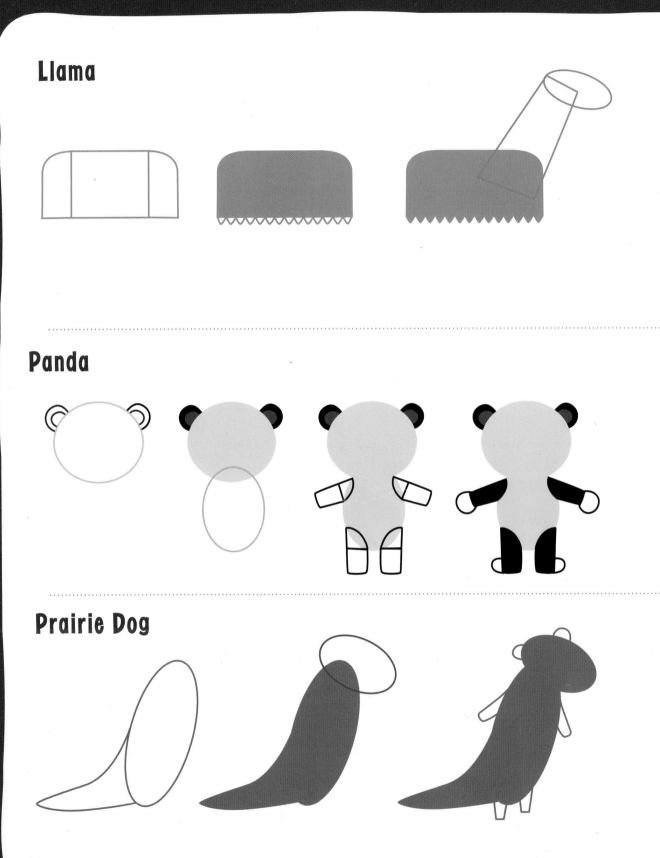

Koala

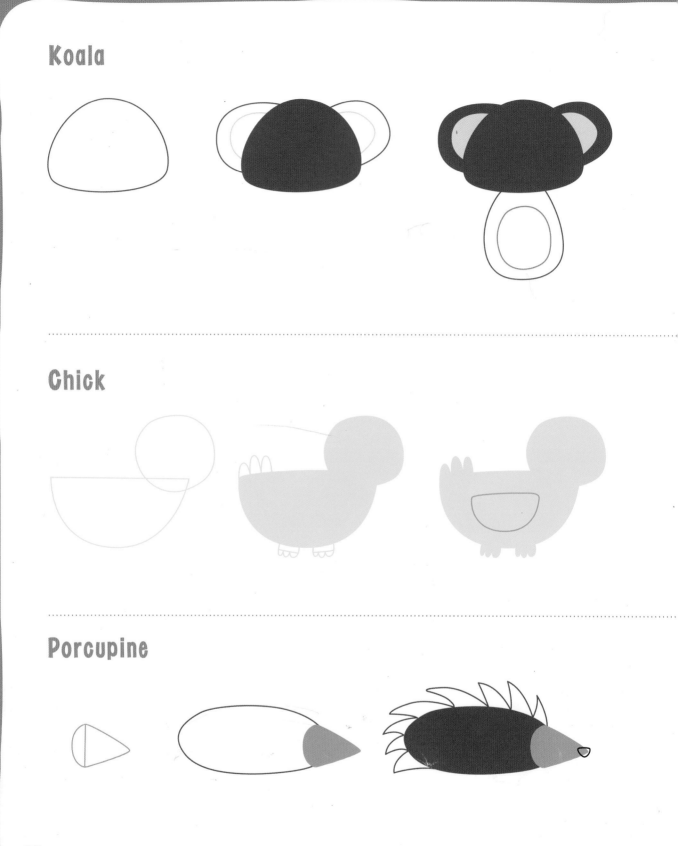

Chick

Porcupine

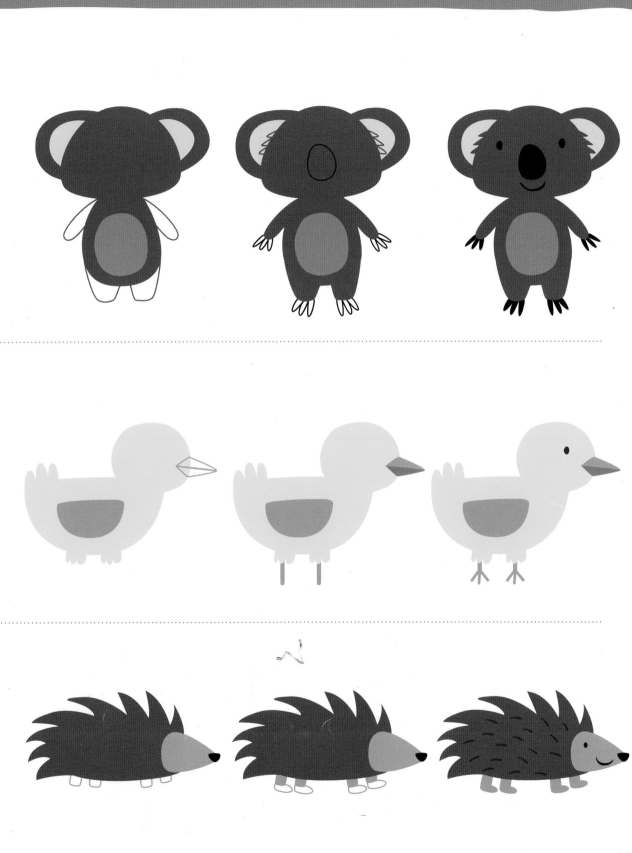

Cowboy Hat

Bamboo

Rocks

Sun

Diving Board

Beach Ball

20

Tree

Palm Tree

Waves

Grass

Clouds

Flowers

Shrub

21

All books published by Picture Window Books
are manufactured with paper containing at least
10 percent post-consumer waste.

Library of Congress Cataloging-in-Publication Data
Ho, Jannie.
  You can draw zoo animals / by Jannie Ho ; illustrated by Jannie Ho.
    p. cm. — (You can draw)
  ISBN 978-1-4048-6275-3 (library binding)
  1. Animals in art—Juvenile literature.
  2. Drawing—Technique—Juvenile literature. I. Ho, Jannie. II. Title.
  NC783.8.Z64B78 2011
  743.6—dc22
                              2010030025

Printed in the United States of America in North Mankato, Minnesota.
092010
005933CGS11

Picture Window Books
151 Good Counsel Drive
P.O. Box 669
Mankato, MN 56002-0669
877-845-8392
www.capstonepub.com

Editor: Shelly Lyons
Designer: Matt Bruning
Art Director: Nathan Gassman
Production Specialist: Sarah Bennett
The illustrations in this book were created digitally.

Internet Sites •

FactHound offers a safe, fun way to find Internet sites related to this book.
All of the sites on FactHound have been researched by our staff.

Here's all you do:

Visit *www.facthound.com*

Type in this code: 9781404862753

Super-cool stuff! Check out projects, games and lots more at
www.capstonekids.com

Look for all the books in the **You Can Draw** series:

YOU CAN DRAW DINOSAURS

YOU CAN DRAW FLOWERS

YOU CAN DRAW MONSTERS AND OTHER SCARY THINGS

YOU CAN DRAW PETS

YOU CAN DRAW PLANES, TRAINS, AND OTHER VEHICLES

YOU CAN DRAW ZOO ANIMALS